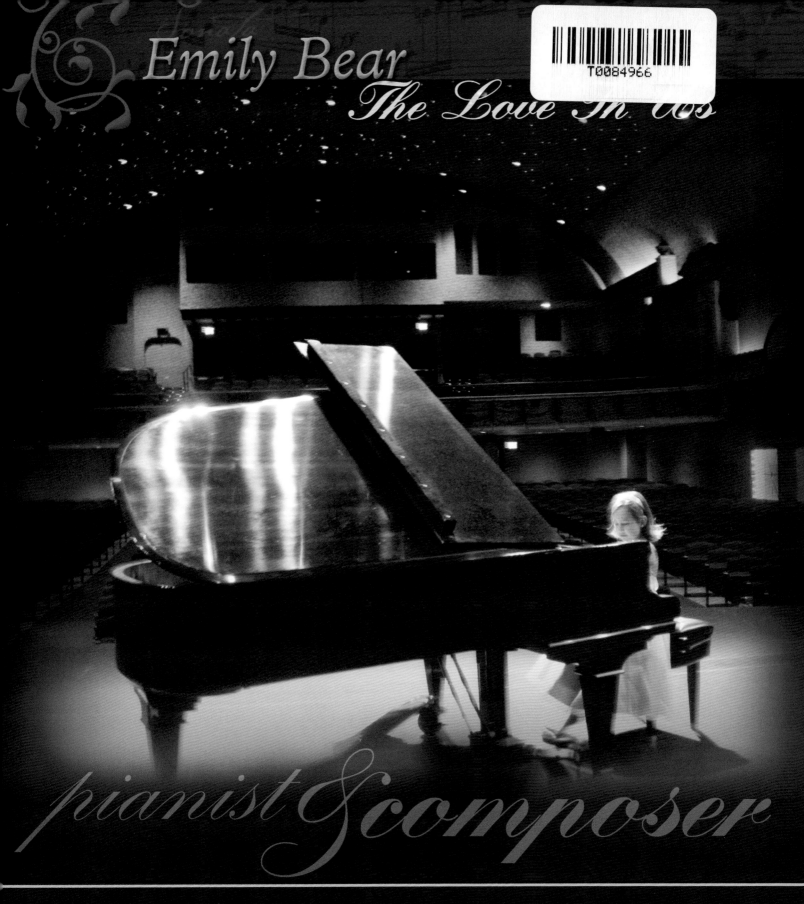

Emily Bear
The Love In Us

pianist&composer

www.emilybear.com

Jordan King Music USA

P.O. Box 271, Rockford, IL 61105

# Table of Contents

*All songs composed by Emily Bear, Age 6*

*All songs composed by Emily Bear, Age 5*

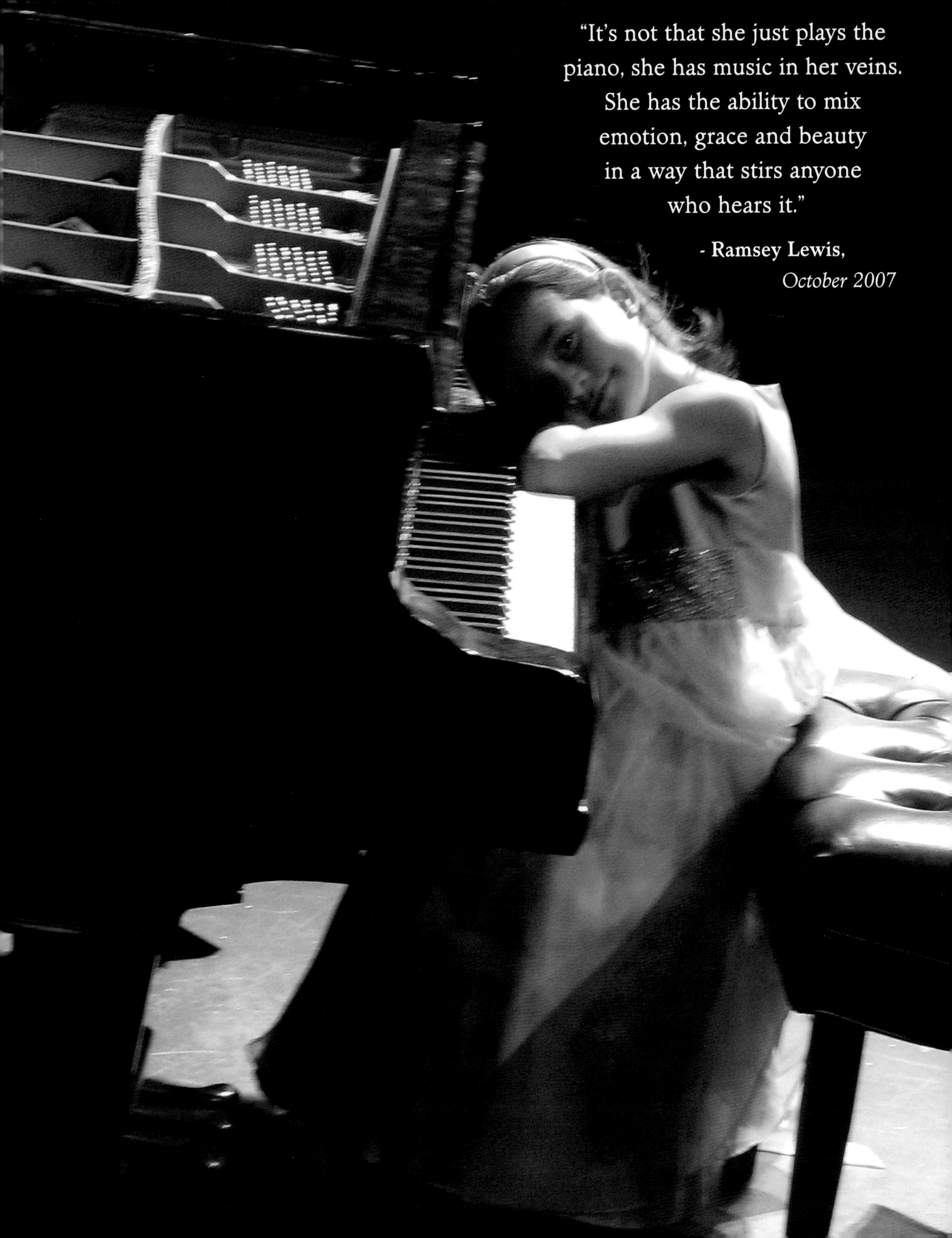

"It's not that she just plays the
piano, she has music in her veins.
She has the ability to mix
emotion, grace and beauty
in a way that stirs anyone
who hears it."

**- Ramsey Lewis,**
*October 2007*

RAMSEY LEWIS TRIO
SPECIAL GUEST EMILY BEAR
OCTOBER 17 730 PM

# Artist Highlights*

We are pleased to share with you this debut
collection of Emily's original songs. This compilation
includes the songs from Emily's second CD, **"The Love In Us"**,
and her original compositions featured on her first CD,
**"Five Years Wise"**. The songs in this collection include
three that were featured on The Ellen Degeneres Show:
*"Ellen's Song"*, *"The Love In Us"* and *"Thanks"*. The songs
from **"Five Years Wise"** were written by Emily when she
was 4 and 5 years old. **"The Love In Us"** CD was
composed at 6 years of age.

This songbook also features the award winning piano solo,
*"Northern Lights"* winner of The **2008 ASCAP
Morton Gould Young Composer Competition Award**.
Emily is the youngest recipient in the
history of the competition.

During the time that these songs were written, Emily
performed a solo concert at **The White House** for
The President and The First Lady, appeared on
**The Ellen Degeneres Show** 3 times, made her
professional debut onstage at **The Ravinia Festival**
and opened for Jazz great, Ramsey Lewis.

The inspiration for these songs came from many directions.
Some were inspired by nature (*"Snowdance"*), a childrens
book on the North Pole (*"Northern Lights"*), a tribute to a
beloved teacher (*"Rosario Sings"*), playing a friends piano
above the clouds on the 54th floor of an apartment building
(*"Piano In The Sky"*). One was a gift (*"Ellen's Song"*) and
one was written at Thanksgiving in appreciation of all
that is good in our world (*"Thanks"*). Whatever the
creative source, she gives us soulful, beautiful
melodies that speak to our emotions.

A portion of the proceeds from the sale of this
songbook, as well as the matching CD's is being
donated to **Susan G. Komen For The Cure**
to help fund research and support for Breast Cancer.

It is Emily's hope that you enjoy playing the
music that has come from her heart.

# Ellen's Song

Music by
EMILY BEAR

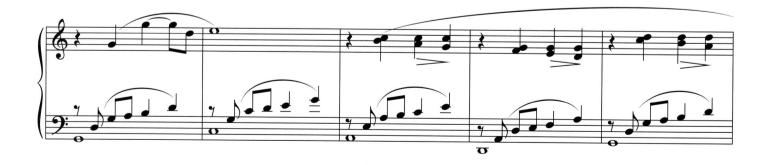

Songs courtesy of Jordan King Music USA (ASCAP).

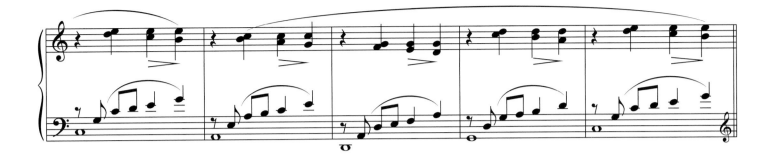

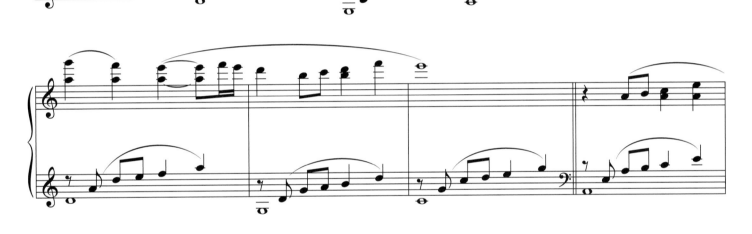

# Thanks

Music by
EMILY BEAR

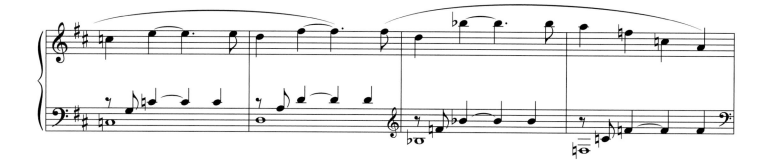

**Poco più mosso**

# The Love In Us

Music by
EMILY BEAR

**Moderately** ♩ = 120

*espressivo*

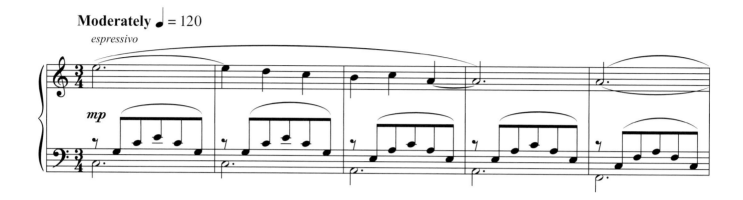

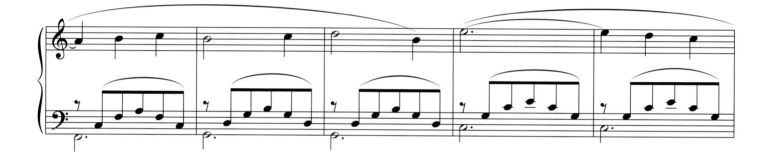

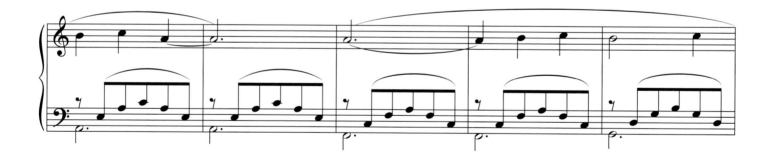

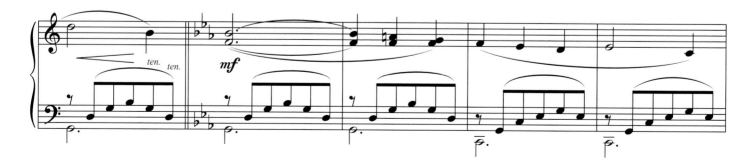

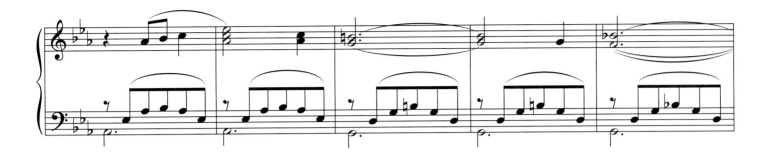

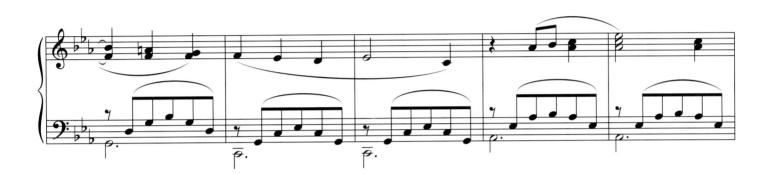

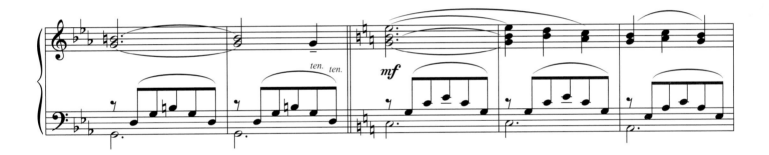

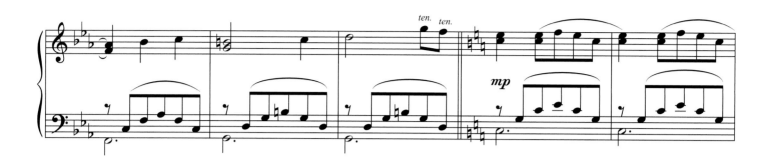

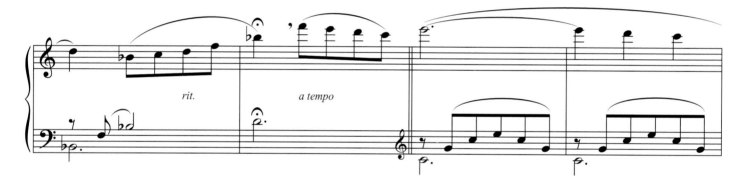

# Spiñata

Music by
EMILY BEAR

Songs courtesy of Jordan King Music USA  (ASCAP).

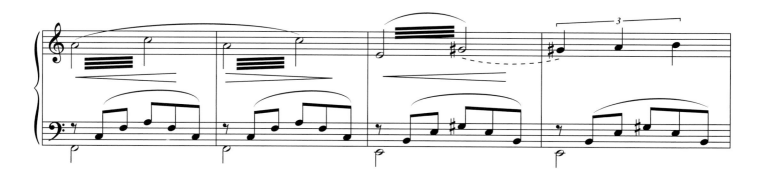

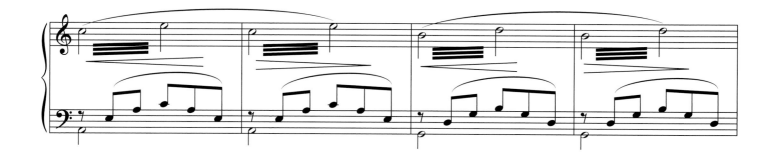

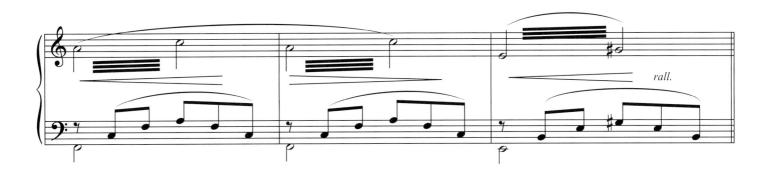

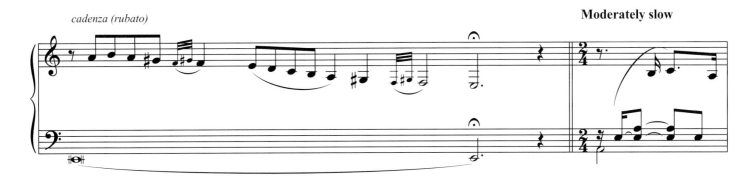

*cadenza (rubato)*

**Moderately slow**

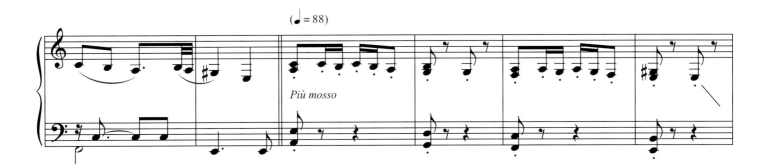

($\quad = 88$)

*Più mosso*

# Journey To My Heart

Music by
EMILY BEAR

Moderately ♩ = 72

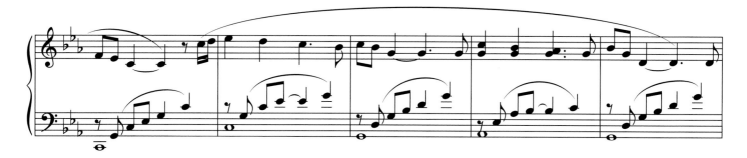

# Snowdance

Music by
EMILY BEAR

**Moderately** ♩ = 66

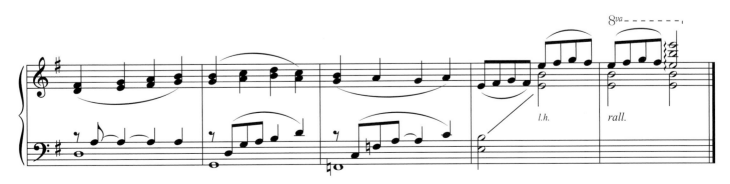

# Piano In The Sky

Music by
EMILY BEAR

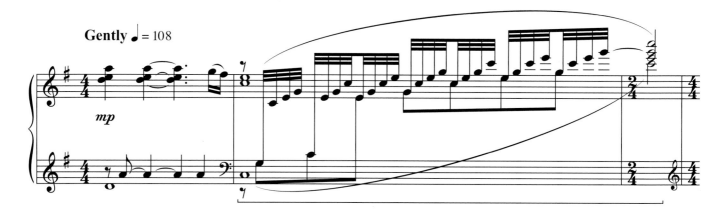

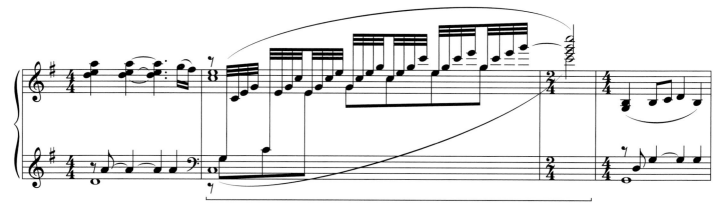

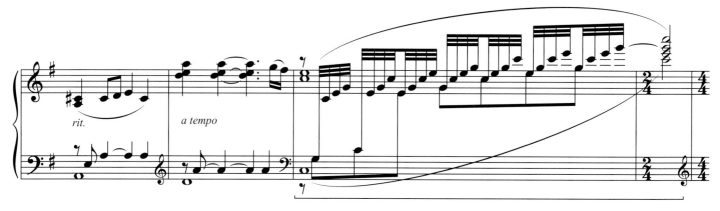

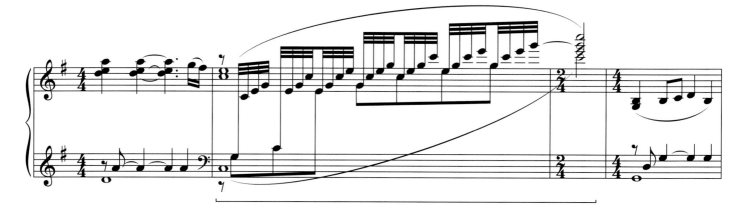

Songs courtesy of Jordan King Music USA (ASCAP).

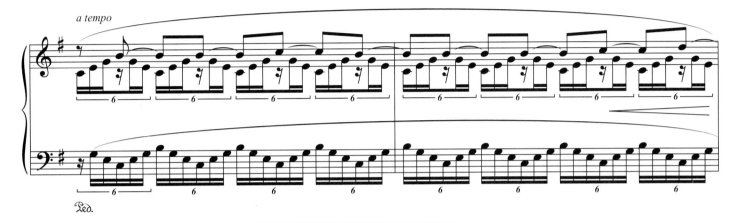

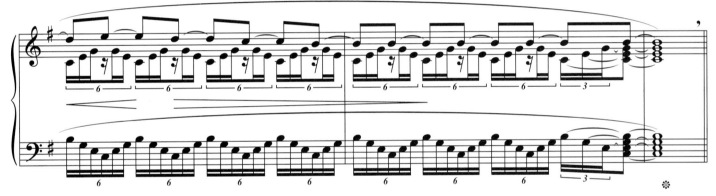

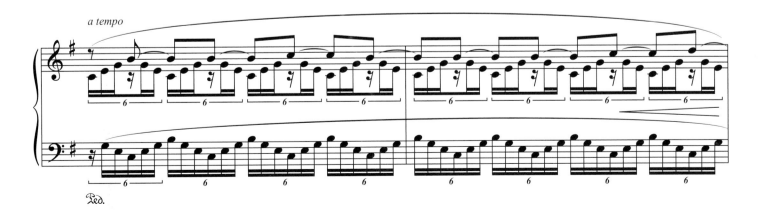

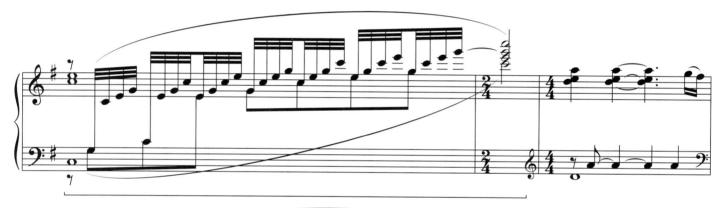

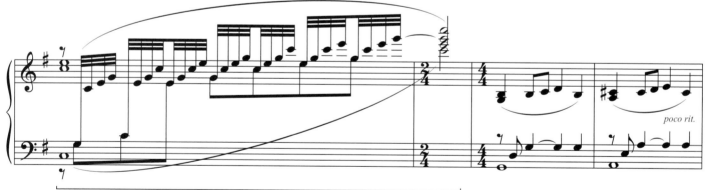

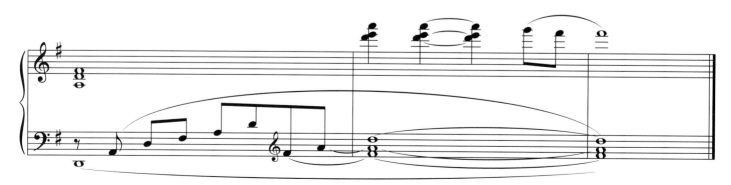

# Freestyle

Music by
EMILY BEAR

**Moderately** ♩ = 72

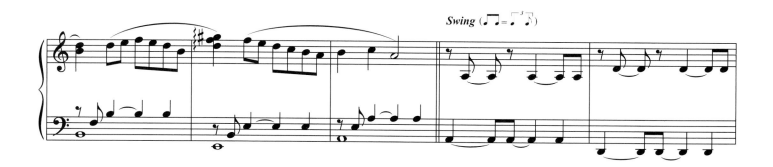

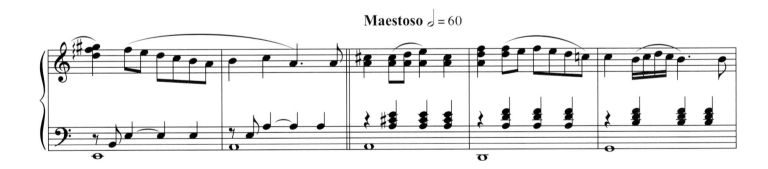

**Maestoso** ♩ = 60

# Northern Lights

Music by
EMILY BEAR

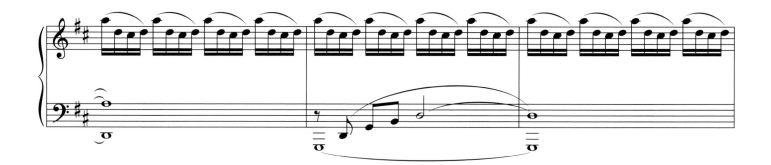

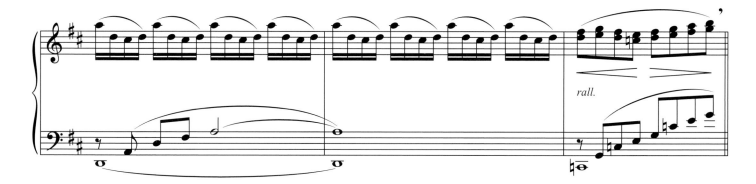

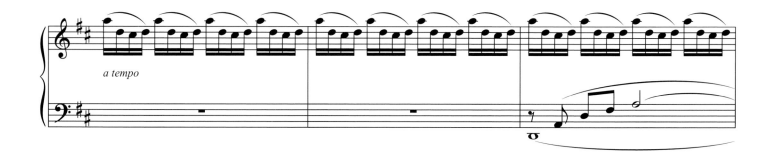

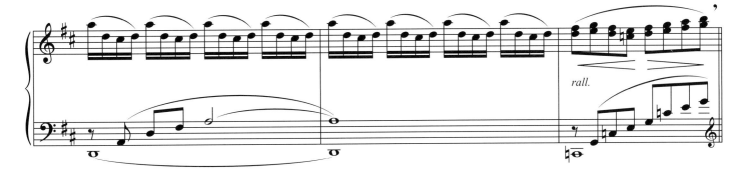

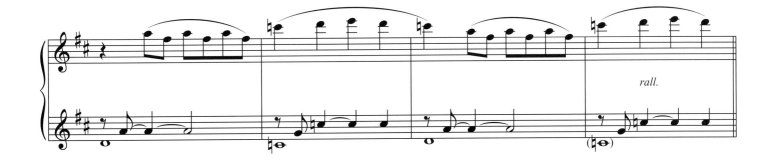

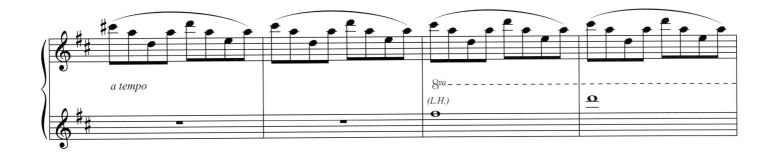

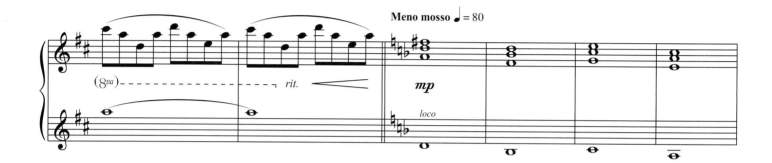

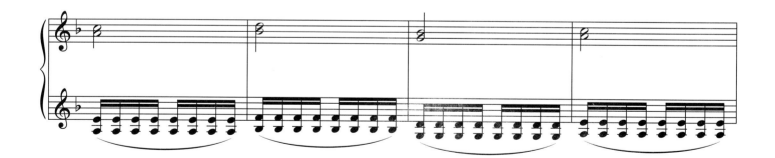

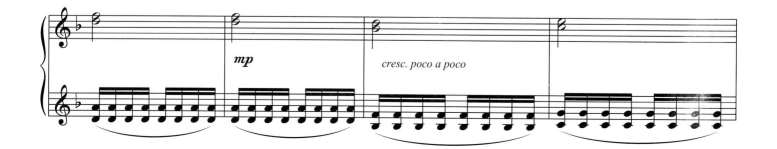

28

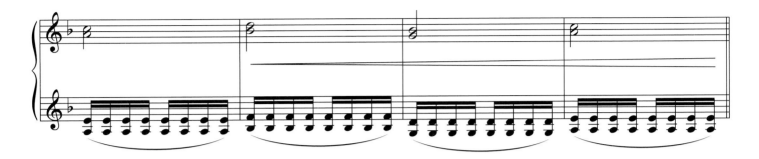

**Doppio movimento** (♩ = ♩)

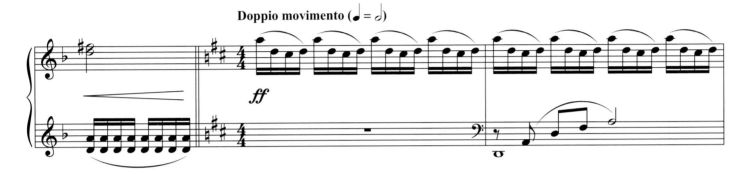

*ff*

*Graziosamente*

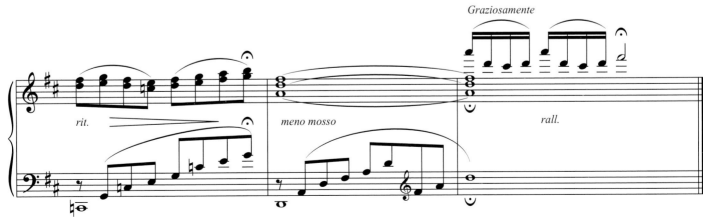

*rit.*          *meno mosso*          *rall.*

# Rosario Sings

Music by
EMILY BEAR

**Moderately** ♩ = 56

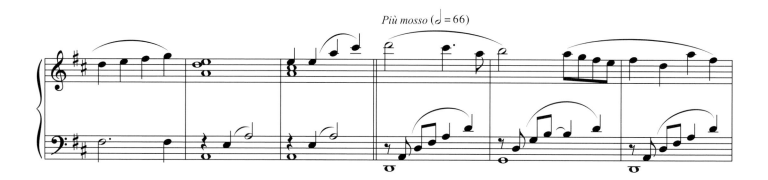

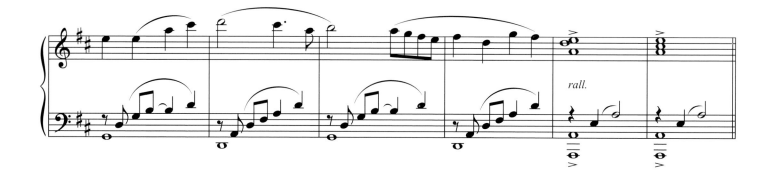

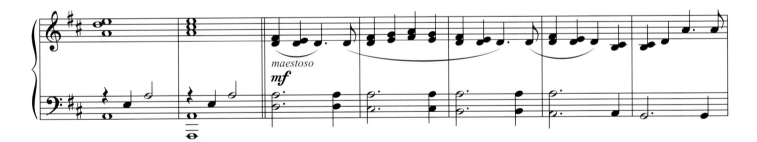

# Rosario Sings

### with vocals

Lyrics by
ANDREA BEAR

Music by
EMILY BEAR

Moderately ♩ = 56

Ev - ery time I sit and play I feel him with me in my fin - gers.

As I play, I think of what he means _____ to me.

Then the mu - sic pours from me and takes me on a jour - ney _____ to an -

oth - er place. A place where he'll still be. He gives me

*Più mosso* (♩ = 66)

joy through my hands, as____ they cre - ate a mel - o -

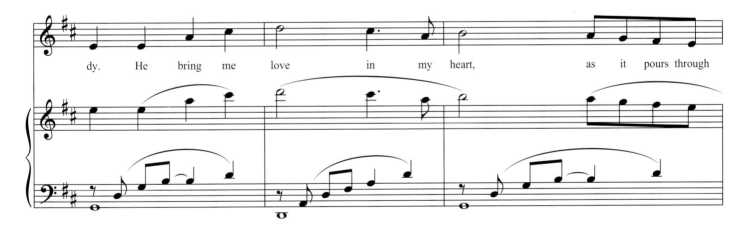

dy. He bring me love in my heart, as it pours through

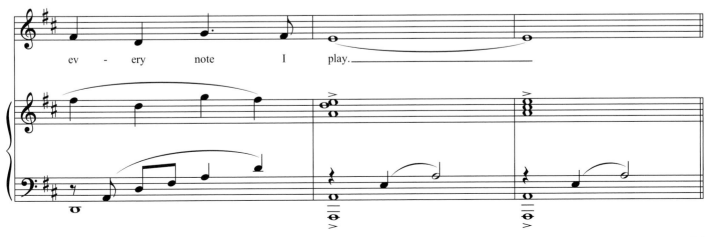

ev - ery note I play.____

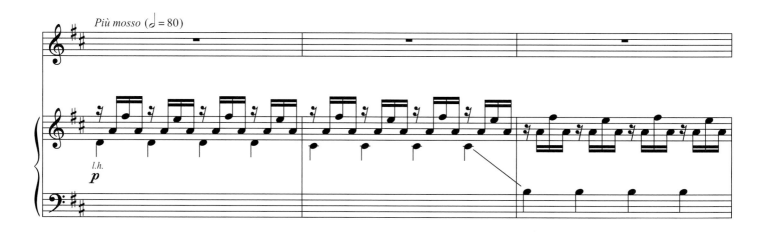

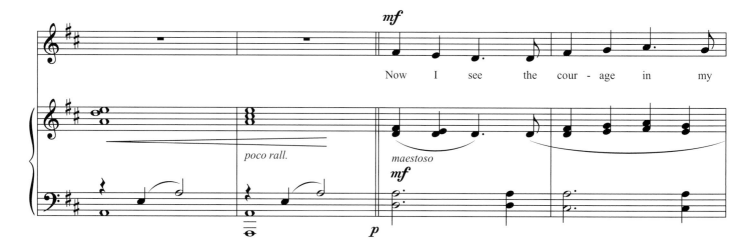

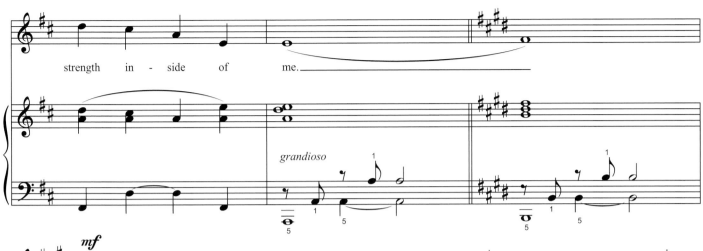

strength in - side of me.

When I play, I share with oth - ers

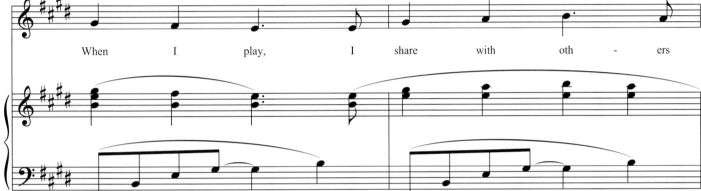

all the joy and love in - side that's in my heart and now I know he

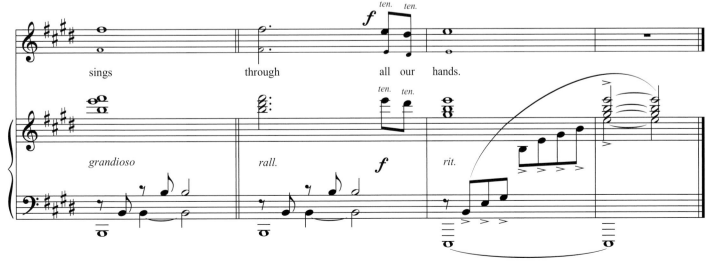

sings through all our hands.

## Five Years Wise

*All songs composed by Emily Bear, Age 5*

# Sunday Morning

Music by
EMILY BEAR

*let ring throughout*

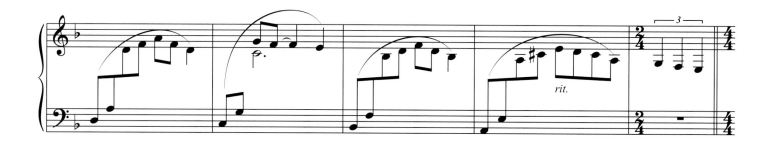

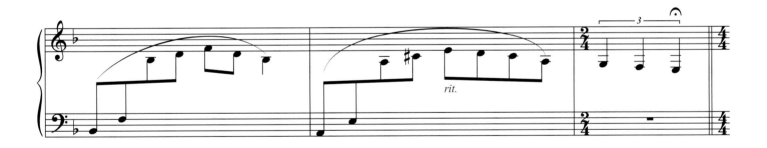

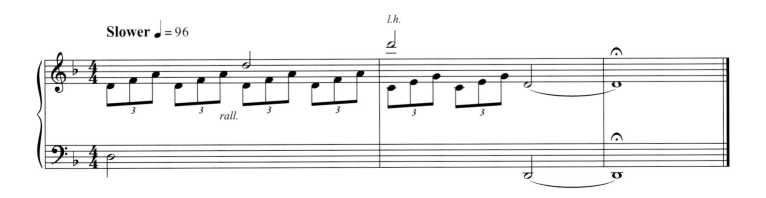

# Silent Option

Lyrics by
ANDREA BEAR

Music by
EMILY BEAR

Ev - 'ry time I think a - bout you; won - der where you are and where you'll be. Ev - 'ry night I sit and won - der what would be and where I'm go - ing. Is my life sup - posed to be this way? Then I think how I want you,

© 2007 Emily Bear. All rights reserved.
Songs courtesy of Jordan King Music USA (ASCAP).

think how I need you, think how I love you so. Then I

think how you left me, think how you hurt me, think how I want you

so, and I cry._____

I need you.

# Pharoah's Sorrow

Lyrics by
ANDREA BEAR

Music by
EMILY BEAR

There, where the seas di‑vide. There, where our worlds col‑lide. We will fight for our pride; all of us strong.

Wave af‑ter wave of an‑ger and pain

filled with the sor - row of our fa - thers for us. We will u - nite and reach up for the stars

all of us now as one. Then we will jour - ney far. Guid - ed by

*rit.*                *a tempo*

one bright star. We now know who we are. All of us to live as one in peace.

*rit.*

# Little Angels

Music by
EMILY BEAR

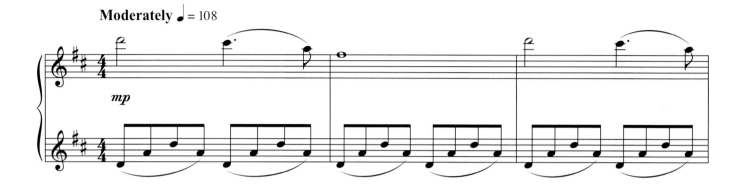

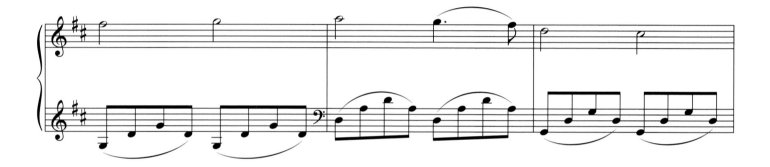

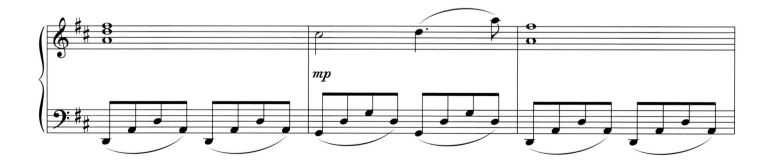

**Tempo I** ♩ = 108

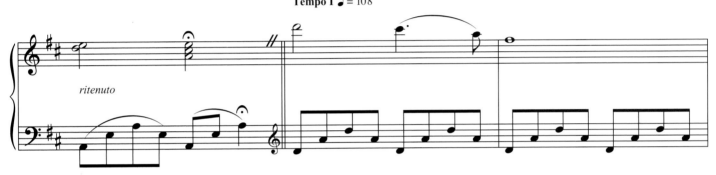

*ritenuto*

*ritenuto*

# Waterlights

Music by
EMILY BEAR

**Moderately** ♩ = 84

**Slower** ♩ = 66

**Tempo primo** ♩ = 84

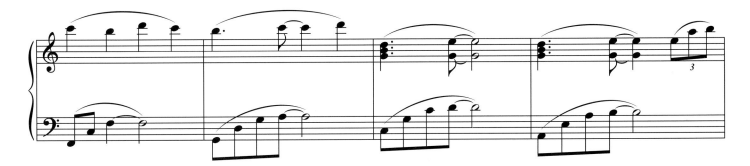

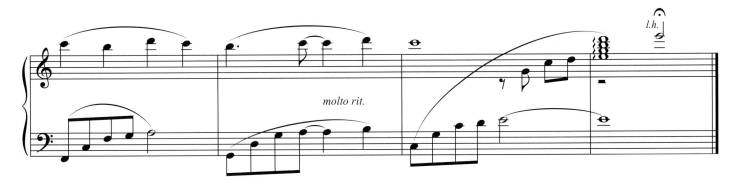

# Rosario Sings

Music by Emily Bear　✣　Lyrics by Andrea Bear

Every time I sit and play
I feel him with me in my fingers.
As I play, I think of what he means to me.

Then the music pours from me
And takes me on a journey
To another place.
A place where he'll still be.

He gives me joy through my hands,
As they create a melody.
He brings me love in my heart,
As it pours through every note I play.

Now I see the courage in my life
To reach for things I dream of
When I feel his strength inside of me.

When I play, I share with others
All the joy and love inside
That's in my heart
And now I know
He sings through all our hands.

✣

Book Design by: Bill Edmundson and Andrea Bear

Photos by: Andrea Bear

www.emilybear.com